Streatham

IN OLD PHOTOGRAPHS

Streatham High Road, looking towards the police station from the High Road junction with Mitcham Lane, *c.* 1907.

Streatham

IN OLD PHOTOGRAPHS

Compiled by PATRICK LOOBEY
and JOHN W. BROWN

*P. J. Loobey
Feb 96*

Alan Sutton Publishing Limited
Phoenix Mill · Far Thrupp · Stroud
Gloucestershire

First Published 1993

Pictures copyright © P.J. Loobey, 1993
Text copyright © John W. Brown, 1993

British Library Cataloguing in Publication
Data

Loobey, Patrick
Streatham in Old Photographs
I. Title II. Brown, John W.
942.165

ISBN 0-7509-0519-0

Typeset in 9/10 Sabon.
Typesetting and origination by
Alan Sutton Publishing Limited.
Printed in Great Britain by
Redwood Books, Trowbridge.

PATRICK LOOBEY, born in 1947, has lived in Balham, Putney, Southfields and Streatham – all within the Borough of Wandsworth. He joined Wandsworth Historical Society in 1969 and has served on its archaeological, publishing and management committees, being chairman of the society in 1991 and 1992. Having collected Edwardian postcards of Wandsworth Borough and the surrounding district for eighteen years, he has a wide-ranging collection encompassing many local roads and subjects.

Patrick has privately published a volume of postcard views of Putney and Roehampton in 1988 and another of Battersea in 1990. Reproductions of all the views in this book are available from Patrick Loobey, 231 Mitcham Lane, Streatham, London, SW16 6PY (081 769 0072).

JOHN W. BROWN has lived in Streatham all his life. His family has a long association with the area dating back to the 1880s, when his great grandfather, John Brown, moved to what was then a semi-rural country town on the outskirts of London.

His interest in local history was aroused when researching his family tree, in response to pleas for help from relatives in America, who were keen to learn about their roots in the UK. His fascination with the subject was encouraged by his father, Leslie Brown, who, when recalling his childhood adventures in the area at the time of the First World War, spoke of a locality which bore little resemblance to the Streatham of today.

John has written a number of books on the history of Streatham and the surrounding area and also publishes reprints of classic histories of the region written in the eighteenth and nineteenth centuries. He is a member of the Local History Group of Streatham Society and the Southwark and Lambeth Archaeological Society and regularly gives talks on the history of Streatham.

Contents

Tate Library, Streatham, *c.* 1899.

Streatham High Road, looking down 'the dip' from near St Leonard's church, *c.* 1906.

Introduction

The truth of the old adage that 'A picture is worth a thousand words' is no more evident than in the following collection of more than 280 fascinating photographs of old Streatham. It paints a picture of times gone by that would be difficult, if not impossible, to put into words.

Most of the views date from the 1890s through to the years immediately prior to the First World War, a period that saw Streatham change from a quiet semi-rural town into a bustling, fashionable London suburb.

Streatham's three railway stations provided excellent connections to the City, and its reputation as a select residential area ensured its popularity with commuters. In fields where once cows grazed and crops grew, the Victorian and Edwardian developers erected roads of large terraced houses that provided comfortable homes for the aspiring middle classes of the day.

These photographs depict the area in the halcyon days of Edwardian England, when ladies strolled the Streatham streets with parasols and young boys in sailor suits played with large hoops – an age when the fastest traveller along the High Road was a cyclist passing a horse and cart, and where local traders decked the streets in bunting and banners to attract Christmas shoppers.

A glimpse of a less affluent Streatham can also be seen, from the young children picking blackberries on the Common to the old crossing sweeper resting from his labours by Streatham station. All human life is here, with each picture having its own tale to tell.

Limitations of space have prevented me from providing anything but the briefest commentary on the pictures featured. However, those interested in learning more about Streatham's past are warmly invited to come along to the meetings of the Local History Group of the Streatham Society, which are held at 8 p.m. on the first Monday of the month in St Leonard's church hall in Tooting Bec Gardens.

I would be most interested in hearing from any reader of their recollections of bygone Streatham, or of the identity of any relatives or friends discovered among the hundreds of unknown people featured in these views.

I hope you will enjoy your stroll through the Streatham streets of yesteryear as you turn the pages of this book and discover an age that although long past, is still within the childhood memories of some of the area's oldest inhabitants.

John W. Brown
316 Green Lane
Streatham SW16

Hambley House Mansions, Streatham Common, in the 1920s.

SECTION ONE

South Streatham – the High Road

Immanuel church, 1907. The church has been a prominent landmark in South Streatham since the original chapel was erected on this site in 1854. It quickly proved too small to accommodate the rapidly rising population of the area and was substantially enlarged in 1865. All that survives of this building today is the church tower, minus the small spire which was taken down in 1941 due to bomb damage.

Hermitage Bridge Cottages are to the left of this photograph, probably taken during the First World War as a soldier is standing by the porch next to the road sweeper. In the distance, a policeman speaks with an inspector at the tram terminus by Hermitage Bridge, where there was a 6 in gap in the rails forcing passengers to change trams in order to continue their journey to Croydon or Streatham.

Coulthurst Cottages, Nos 357–67 Streatham High Road, *c.* 1906. These old weatherboarded cottages were probably built in the eighteenth century to house agricultural labourers working on Streatham Farm. They were one of the last surviving relics of the old village of Lower Streatham and were demolished in 1954 to make way for a block of council flats.

Streatham High Road, 1919. Heathdene Road, the first turning on the right, had only recently been laid out. Opposite is a row of early Victorian cottages, in one of which lived Edwin 'Dusty' Rhodes, a well-known music-hall comedian of the day.

Arragon Parade, Nos 554–80 Streatham High Road, c. 1912. This parade of early Edwardian shops was erected between Glencairn Road and Guildersfield Road in 1904 to serve the rapidly expanding population inhabiting the recently-built houses in the surrounding streets.

Pendennis College for Girls (*c.* 1910) was located at No. 285 Streatham High Road in the large block of Victorian houses that used to stand between Voss Court and Baldry Gardens. By the 1920s the building was used as the junior department of St Helen's School (see p. 149). After the Second World War these buildings stood neglected for some time before they were eventually demolished and council flats erected on the site.

Laying tram lines in the High Road by Immanuel church, May 1909. Note the wooden road blocks that made up the road surface piled up ready to be relaid when the rails had been installed.

Western Terrace and Church Place, Nos 456–68 Streatham High Road, *c.* 1919. This row of tiny, ancient cottages stood opposite Streatham Common from at least the late eighteenth century. The sailor who steered HMS *Victory* during the Battle of Trafalgar once lived in the one nearest Immanuel church.

Bank Parade, Nos 426–50 Streatham High Road, *c.* 1903. The parade was built in 1890 by Mr Marriage of Croydon, to the designs of Tooly & Son. It was erected on the site of two large houses called Westwell and High Elms. The glass canopy attached to the parade was taken down in 1939, much to the disappointment of pedestrians who used to rush to shelter beneath it during wet weather.

Greyhound Lane junction with Streatham High Road in the early 1920s. The bus inspector's white box can be seen at the centre of the junction, walking towards which are four young cricketers carrying their bat and stumps after a game on the Common.

No. 402 Streatham High Road, *c.* 1912. This house formed part of Bladon Terrace that used to stand between Barrow and Lewin Roads on the site now occupied by advertising hoardings. The photograph was used by Walter Redman Payne to announce to his friends that he had recently moved to this address.

Hambley Mansions, in the foreground, was built in 1877 to the designs of local architect, Sir Ernest George, President of RIBA from 1908–10. The building survives today as Potter and Perrin's, kitchen and bathroom fittings shop. On the far left is the garden of Dr Robert Stewart's house. He was Physician to Queen Adelaide, and lived here from the early 1840s to the mid-1860s.

Bladon Terrace in the 1920s. Originally large terraced houses (see p. 14), by the time this photograph was taken the ground floor of the buildings had been converted to shops. Former residents are said to include Samuel Laing, Postmaster General, and Sir John Milton, Accountant General to the Army, who died here in 1880.

The Congregational church. The above view is dated *c.* 1930, while the lower photograph dates from shortly after the church had been built in 1901. The High Road is still lined with sturdy trees, enhancing the rustic aspect which the road maintained up to the time of the First World War. The church was designed by James Cubitt and the foundation stone was laid by Charles Derry, who lived at Woodlands in Tooting Bec Gardens, and whose family were partners in Derry and Toms, the well-known department store. The church is now the United Reform church.

The view from the tower of the Congregational church in 1913, showing the western slope of Streatham Common. To the left is the house known as The Chimes, so named because of a clock on the outside wall which struck the hours and quarters and whose 'chimes' could be heard for some distance.

Towards Streatham station, before the First World War. One of Streatham's policemen cycles past the Congregational church in the High Road towards the station.

Nos 245–9 Streatham High Road, *c.* 1924. The three large Victorian houses stand on the corner of the High Road and Hopton Road. No. 245 was for many years the Streatham School of Music. The houses were demolished in 1938 and Century House was erected on the site. This was the head office of James Walker's, the jewellers, until 1984 when the building was converted into flats.

Streatham Constitutional Club international bowls match, between club members and players from Australia, Tasmania and New Zealand, 27 May 1907. The club was formed in 1905 and originally occupied the premises in Streatham High Road, which were later demolished to make way for the Streatham Ice Rink.

South Streatham Streets

The Lonesome Mission Hall at the junction of Lilian and Marion Roads, 1907. The hall was erected by members of Streatham Baptist church in 1887. Commonly known as 'the tin tabernacle' because of its corrugated iron structure, it cost £200 to build. Workers would visit the mission from Streatham in groups of six or seven, carrying storm lanterns to guide them through the mud and ditches of the trackway to Lonesome, now Streatham Vale, making sure that at least one of their party was a 'burly fellow' so that they could resist any possible attack from the locals.

Members of the Hibbert family, outside Sunnyside, No. 6 Arragon Gardens, 1907. Building work began in 1900 in what was originally known as Arragon Street and then Arragon Avenue. However, in 1904 it was decided to call the road Arragon Gardens, which was more to the liking of the residents.

Abercairn Road in the early 1930s. Typical of the Streatham Vale Estate, this road was developed in the 1920s to provide comfortable homes with all 'mod cons'. Flt. Lt. Stanley Taylor DFM and DFC and bar, one of the most decorated veterans of the RAF pathfinder squadrons in the Second World War, lived here in the 1930s and '40s.

Barrow Road, *c.* 1919. These old weatherboarded cottages stood near the High Road end of Barrow Road, and are thought to date back to the eighteenth century when the road was known as Bakers Lane. Opposite them used to stand Oakfield House, which contained a 'lock up' room with barred doors, in which vagrant and disorderly persons in South Streatham used to be detained. These buildings were demolished in the mid-1930s to make way for the erection of blocks of flats.

Braxted Park, *c.* 1912. This road was originally called Braxted Road, the name being changed in 1906 to more accurately commemorate the property held in Essex by the then landowners, the Du Cane family.

Bridgewood Road when development commenced, *c.* 1928. The houses have only recently been built and the road and pavements have yet to be made up. As a temporary measure, railway sleepers have been laid out to provide vehicles with a firm surface on which to drive.

Buckleigh Road, *c.* 1914. Most of these large Victorian houses were built in the 1880s. Ellen Warrington, whose painting of The Rookery Gardens was selected by Princess Mary for the design of her 1921 Christmas card, lived at No. 48.

Colmer Road, *c.* 1912. Colmer, Wellington and Wolseley Terraces were erected in this road by 1867, with further building being completed by the end of the nineteenth century. No. 1 Colmer Road was the home of James Baker, horse slaughterer. William Shepherd, at one time the oldest bell-ringer in England, lived at No. 32 from where he journeyed to the Immanuel bell tower every Sunday until well into his 80s.

Copley Park (*c.* 1911) commemorates the family name of the wife of Sir Charles Du Cane, her father taking up the title Lord Lyndhurst when he was made a lord. The Du Cane family owned the land on which the road was laid out in 1906. Sir Edward Hodgson, President of the International Bowling Association and the English Bowling Association, lived here until his death in 1955.

Eardley Road, *c.* 1906 (above) and *c.* 1910 (below). Originally an extension of Ellison Road, Eardley Road was renamed in honour of the Revd Stenton Eardley, the first vicar of Immanuel church, who served the parish from 1854–83. Streatham Common station can be seen in the centre of the top picture. Captain L.D. Chidson MC lived at No. 13. A former Westminster Abbey chorister, he won his Military Cross in 1916 for 'great gallantry' and was killed in action in France in the following year.

Fontaine Road, c. 1915. Work on the fine Edwardian houses which line this road began in 1902 when it was known as Fontaine Street, the name being changed in 1907. Cal McCord, the famous post-war radio cowboy, lived here in the 1950s and used to fascinate local children with his lasso tricks.

Glencairn Road, c. 1912. Building commenced at the High Road end of Glencairn Road in 1900 and continued intermittently over the next quarter of a century as the different style of houses in the road show. The Revd Isaac Dunbar lived here. He was head of the Church Mission to the Jews in Tunis in the Second World War, suffered bombing from the RAF, the *Luftwaffe*, the Italians and the Americans, and also undertook a daring escape from capture by the Nazis in 1942.

Green Lane, *c.* 1912. The lane is an ancient trackway leading from Streatham to Thornton Heath. Lined with fine old trees and thick hedges, it remained 'green' well into the 1920s when Wates (the builders) began to develop the area for housing. The picture below shows the entrance to the North Surrey Golf Club, part of the grounds of which survives today as Norbury Park. The footpath on the left marked the Streatham parish boundary with Croydon that now runs along the bottom of the back gardens of the houses in Strathbrook Road.

Guildersfield Road (above, *c.* 1910) was laid out on the grounds of Guildersfield House, on what is probably the site of the 'Guilder's Field' of South Streatham, a tract of arable land cultivated by the 'Guild men' or villeins of the middle ages. St Andrew's church (below, *c.* 1905) was erected in 1886 to the designs of local architect Sir Ernest George, and the adjoining vicarage was built in 1889. Sadly, the church was destroyed by fire in the early hours of 10 March 1992 and now stands derelict.

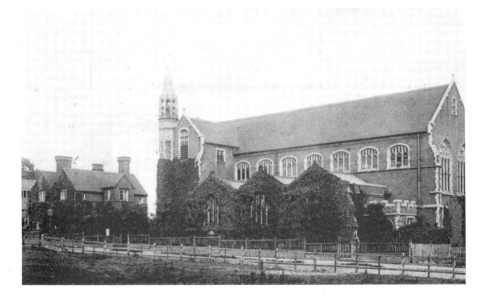

Greyhound Lane follows the route of an ancient trackway leading from Streatham to Mitcham, via Lonesome, an apt name which described the area centred at the end of Streatham Vale up to the First World War. The top picture shows the High Road end of the lane in 1907. The bottom view shows the inter-war houses erected on the site of Greyhound Lane Farm and the Immanuel Mission Room at the junction with Pathfield Road (see p. 32). The Mission Room was built in 1899 and replaced an old wooden hut which served as the Baptist chapel. Immanuel sold the mission premises in 1935 and used the proceeds to build a hall next to the church.

Greyhound Lane junction with Ellison Road, *c*. 1910. The Railway Tavern stands on the right hand corner. The tavern was known locally as Laceby's, after Coulson Laceby, the publican, who was also Streatham's senior member on Wandsworth Council.

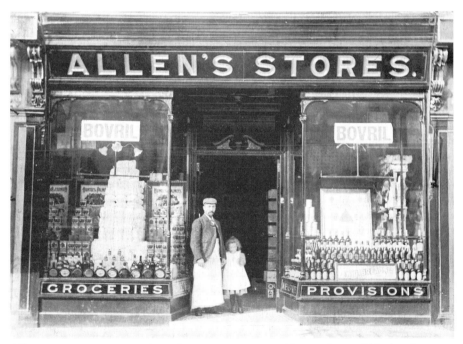

Allen's Stores, No. 15 Greyhound Lane, *c*. 1912. Mr Allen and one of his daughters are standing in the doorway in the centre of a magnificent display of groceries, provisions and bottled beer and wine.

Kempshott Road, *c.* 1907. Although this road was laid out in 1866, most of the original buildings date from the 1880s, with the odd-numbered houses between the High Road and Buckleigh Road originally built as Albion Villas. Douglas Cow, of the Indian Rubber company P.B. Cows, lived at No. 8. He was arrested on Westminster Bridge in 1888 on suspicion of being Jack the Ripper, but on providing an impeccable alibi he was subsequently released from custody.

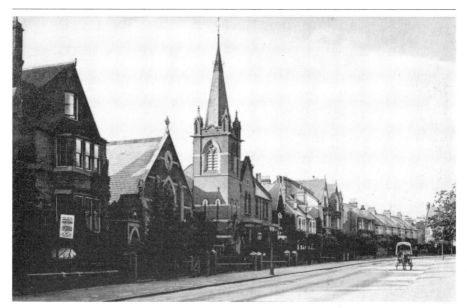

Lewin Road, *c.* 1906. The top picture shows Streatham Baptist church (see p. 32). The road was laid out in 1872, being named after Benjamin Lewin, who was buried in St Leonard's churchyard in 1794. His gravestone describes him as 'a man greatly respected by all who had the pleasure of his acquaintance'. No. 17 was built in 1884 for the headmaster of Streatham School and has the motto 'Small but suited to the Master' over the door. At No. 59 lived C.F. Crawford, Bridgemaster to the City of London, and W. Woodington, sculptor, died at No. 92 in 1922. He worked with his father on the relief of the Battle of the Nile, which adorns the base of Nelson's Column in Trafalgar Square.

Streatham Baptist church provides a prominent landmark at the top of Lewin Road. Built in 1877 and extended in 1901, the church supercedes an old wooden hut on wheels which the Streatham Baptists used to hold their services at different places around the parish before it finally rested at the top of Greyhound Lane (see p. 28).

SECTION THREE

Streatham Common, The Rookery and Norwood Grove

Streatham Scouts practice their woodcraft and first aid on the Common while a group of new recruits look on in 1910. To the left of the Scouts a young boy stands holding a large rounders bat. The wood at the top of the Common was a favourite spot for local children who established 'secret' camps in the thick undergrowth. The wood is a comparatively recent development having been established during the closing years of the nineteenth century. In the mid-1800s the area at the top of the Common was thick with gorse and bushes, but devoid of trees.

Streatham High Road, 1914. This view from the top of Immanuel church tower shows passing horse carts making good use of the water trough at the foot of Streatham Common. The trough was relocated to this spot from Streatham Hill in 1895, where it was erected in 1880 by W. Ward of Lawn House, Brixton. Following the widening of the High Road, the trough was moved to the top of the Common, opposite the tea-room, in 1974. The young horse-chestnuts seen here at the foot of the Common are now fine mature trees.

Relaxing on the Common, c. 1912. Streatham Common has always been a popular spot for Sunday strolls and it was fashionable in Edwardian times for mothers and nannies to take their children there to enjoy the fresh air.

Cricket on the Common, *c*. 1916. Popular in the nineteenth and early twentieth centuries, local gentlemen used to play the game wearing black top hats. For many years the Streatham Cricket Club had a pitch roped off on the bottom half of the Common to protect the wicket, and there are a number of incidents recorded of innocent people enjoying a quiet stroll being knocked unconscious by cricket balls.

Blackberrying, *c*. 1913. When the area at the top of Streatham Common was covered in a thick growth of blackberry bushes, blackberrying was a popular activity, particularly with children.

The Ponds in the early 1900s. Before the London County Council installed children's paddling ponds at the top and bottom of Streatham Common, natural ponds occupied the sites and provided drinking water for the livestock which used to graze nearby. The upper pond, above, was known locally as Coster's Pond, after James Coster who used to live opposite in Hill House, the entrance gates of which can be seen on the left hand side of the photograph. The lower pond, below, was very deep and a favourite spot for local suicides.

The Rookery, *c.* 1912. Built in 1786, The Rookery replaced an earlier building erected in 1732. Previously known as Streatham Wells, or the Well House, it marks the site of the mineral wells, which attracted large numbers of visitors to Streatham in the eighteenth century. The house can be seen on the left of the photograph above, taken shortly before it was acquired in 1912 by the London County Council. The LCC demolished the building and developed the grounds as a public garden (below), which was opened to the public in the summer of 1913.

The White Garden (*c*. 1914) was a popular attraction at The Rookery and a favourite spot which Queen Mary used to visit each summer. The garden was planned so that it provided a continual vista of white blooms throughout the summer months.

The Wishing Well (1920s) marks the site where visitors used to come to take the Streatham waters. When the gardens were opened to the public it took on a new role as a wishing well, with present-day visitors throwing coins in the water for good luck.

The Avenue, *c*. 1914. On Sundays a steady stream of strollers would journey along this favourite promenade between The Rookery Gardens and Norwood Grove. The drive used to provide the carriage entrance to Norwood Grove, and the gateposts and the gatekeeper's lodge still survive today.

Norwood Grove in the early 1930s. Probably built in the opening years of the nineteenth century, only the eastern half of the building survives today. It was formerly the residence of Arthur Anderson, founder of the P & O shipping line, and also of Frederick Nettleford, whose family business now forms part of the GKN group. Note the sphinxes flanking the steps leading down to the gardens on the right hand side of the house.

The Mission School for Hebrew children, *c*. 1905. The school stood on Streatham Common Southside. As well as providing Christian education for some eighty Jewish children, the school was a residential home for Jews who had converted to Christianity. Originally a large house built around 1775, it became the Collegiate School in 1855 and then Immanuel College. The building was enlarged in 1895 and was subsequently acquired by the London County Council and became the Southside Home. It was demolished in 1988 and the site was redeveloped in 1993 as a nursing home for the elderly.

Newlands, 17 Streatham Common Northside, *c*. 1906. The house was formerly the home of Mr and Mrs W.L. Field, who tragically lost all five of their sons in the opening twelve months of the First World War. Newlands Court now stands on the site.

Northerndene, 20 Streatham Common Northside, *c.* 1908. One of the few large houses still standing in the area, Northerndene was built around 1873 and extended in 1878. It was the former home of George Pratt, the founder of the Streatham department store which bore his name. Note the adjoining coach-house that also survives today, and incorporates the initials JR in an attractive motif above the upper windows.

Park Hill Lodge, *c.* 1904. Visible from the top of the Common, the lodge guards the entrance to the large mansion that survives today as St Michael's Convent. This handsome house was formerly the residence of Sir Henry Tate, of Tate & Lyle sugar fame, who founded the Tate Gallery. He was a generous benefactor to Streatham, presenting the parish with its first free public library. It was his custom to open his gallery at Park Hill once a year so that local residents could enjoy his paintings.

Benhurst, *c.* 1911. This large imposing house stood at the junction of Streatham Common Northside and Leigham Court Road. It was formerly the residence of Dr Canon Carver, headmaster of Dulwich College. It was demolished in 1934 and Benhurst Court erected on the site.

Esam Lodge (*c.* 1908) stood between Leigham Court Road and Crown Lane Gardens and is commemorated today in the local street name Esam Way. The house was owned by William Bell, who died there in 1930 at the age of 84. He was chairman of Beck and Co., a Southwark engineering company, and during his life he amassed a large fortune, most of which he left to his servants as he had no family.

Crown Lane, *c.* 1910. In the opening years of the twentieth century this route leading from Streatham to Upper Norwood was but a quiet country lane.

The British Home and Hospital for Incurables, *c.* 1906. This establishment moved from its previous premises in Clapham to its present site in Crown Lane in 1894, when the new hospital was officially opened by the Prince and Princess of Wales on 3 July. It is shown before the Alexandra Wing was added to the western end of the building in 1913.

SECTION FOUR
The First World War

Streatham War Memorial, *c.* 1927. Designed by Albert T. Toft, the memorial was unveiled by General Sir Charles Monro before a gathering of some five thousand people on Saturday 14 October 1922. It stands in the centre of the Garden of Remembrance, and originally commemorated the 720 inhabitants of Streatham who gave their lives in the First World War. It was subsequently also dedicated to the fallen of the Second World War at a ceremony performed by the Mayor of Wandsworth, Councillor Ronald Ash, on Sunday 8 May 1959.

The United Services Club. Money raised for the Streatham War Memorial also covered the cost of the purchase of The Chimes, the large house seen in the top photograph, c. 1933, overlooking the Garden of Remembrance. This was used as a social centre for war veterans and was known as the United Services Club. The house had formerly been the home of Sir Horace Brooks Marshall, Lord Mayor of London in 1918–19. The club had to be demolished following damage caused by a flying bomb in the Second World War and part of Albert Carr Gardens was erected on the site, as can be seen in the lower photograph, taken after the war.

Members of the Volunteer Training Corps at their Whitsun training camp, 1915. Eardley Road Drill Hall had been the base of the 2nd Volunteer Battalion of the East Surrey Regiment long before the First World War. However, with the outbreak of hostilities, a large number of local men joined the Volunteer Training Corps, which was also based at the drill hall.

The funeral procession of tram conductor Charles Boys and motorman T. Gaymer, 29 September 1916. Both men were based at the Telford Avenue Tram Depot and were among the thirteen people who lost their lives during an air raid on Streatham, one of only twenty-five places in London to suffer such an attack during the First World War. The air raid took place on 24 September 1916 when a Zeppelin dropped a number of bombs while flying over the area. One fell at Streatham Hill destroying a tram car. A further thirty-three people were injured in the attack.

SECTION FIVE

Central Streatham

Streatham station bridge, 1908. Christmas shoppers to Streatham were greeted by this notice strung across the road outside Streatham station as part of the Christmas decorations put up by local traders. Note the crossing sweeper resting by the right hand banner pole.

Queen's Parade, *c.* 1910. Built in 1885, Queen's Parade, seen here on the right, is much older than the modern lines of the building would suggest. It remains little changed today.

781   *STREATHAM. — High Road. — LL.*

Station Parade, *c.* 1906. The row of small lock-up shops leading from the High Road entrance to Streatham station to Station Approach were demolished in 1984 to make way for a supermarket. Note the young boy in his sailor's uniform in the foreground.

The Gleneagle Road junction with Streatham High Road, looking southwards towards Streatham station, 1905.

Turner's Job and Post Master's in the early 1900s. At the rear of this building, seen here on the right, was stabling for forty coach horses. Residents frequently complained about the noise of the coachman's horns, forewarning the stable boys of their arrival.

Ayers & Ayers, 1910. This firm of estate agents was situated at No. 221 Streatham High Road, next to the Bedford Park Hotel, the saloon entrance to which can be seen on the right. The business was operated by two brothers, J.W. and H.G. Ayers, who were the grandsons of John Pettengill, the popular licensee of the Horse and Groom public house, whose family ran the pub from 1854 to 1894.

Streatham Methodist church, c. 1908. Designed by Charles Ball and built in 1882, this imposing building stood at the High Road junction with Stanthorpe Road until it was demolished in 1967. The site is now occupied by an Iceland supermarket.

The hill up to St Leonard's church before the First World War. The overhead power lines for the trams are clearly visible. A lady with a parasol can be seen walking up the hill on the right hand side of road – a rare sight in modern Streatham.

Streatham Green, *c.* 1924. When Lady Kymer enclosed the village green in 1794, the villagers were so incensed that they petitioned the Duke of Bedford, the Lord of the Manor of Streatham and Tooting Bec, to force her to open it up again. About a hundred years later, when the Council enclosed the green with iron railings the event passed without a murmur.

Bedford Row, *c.* 1910. A picturesque row of mid-eighteenth-century cottages used to stand opposite the Streatham Green. Named after the Duke of Bedford, the cottages were demolished in the early 1880s to make way for the row of large Victorian shops, which still occupies the site today.

Nos 270–90 Streatham High Road, *c.* 1906. This block of shops was erected in 1880 and the double-storeyed glass windows of the premises that stood next to the village forge were a well-known local landmark, particularly for passengers travelling on the top of the old horse-drawn buses. The block was demolished in 1932 when the road was widened and a new parade of shops was erected on the site.

Looking down the hill, 1905. The buildings on the left hand side of the High Road have changed little since this photograph was taken. The old row of small double-storeyed shops at the top of the hill are one of the last reminders present-day residents have of the old village of Streatham.

No. 149 Streatham High Road, 1905. At the turn of the twentieth century C. Keevil provided food for the body at this shop at the top of the hill. Today food for the soul is provided from the same premises by the Manna Christian bookshop.

The quiet High Road junction with Mitcham Lane in 1916 (above) and the 1920s (below). Note the original position of the Dyce Fountain prior to its removal to Streatham Green in 1933. This was designed by William Dyce, the famous Streatham artist, and erected by public subscription in 1862 as a tribute to him by the inhabitants of Streatham. In the upper picture the tower of Manor House Lodge can be seen in Mitcham Lane. By the 1920s, the former village forge has been converted to a market hall.

SECTION SIX

Central Streatham

Streets

Tooting Bec Gardens, 1906. Formerly known as Long Road and Streatham Lane, the name of the stretch of road between Streatham High Road and Tooting Bec Common was changed to Tooting Bec Gardens in 1881. The view towards the High Road was dominated by the spires of St Leonard's church and the church of the English Martyrs, which together formed a distinct landmark clearly visible from the surrounding high ground. The entrance to the rectory (see p. 58) is on the left, and the gates to Woodlands on the right.

Streatham Rectory at the turn of the twentieth century. Parts of the old Streatham rectory were thought to date back to at least 1535. It was enlarged and altered several times over the ensuing 350 years. The building was eventually demolished in 1907 to make way for the church hall and a new rectory, which was itself pulled down in 1972. For sixty-one years, from 1843 to 1904, the old rectory was the home of Streatham's longest serving rector, Canon John Nicholl, who died on 10 September 1905 at the age of 96 years.

The Broadway, c. 1914. Most of the shops in this row between Gleneagle Road and Streatham Green were originally built in 1884. Damage caused to the buildings by the Zeppelin raid on Streatham in 1916 can still be seen today on the plaque above No. 322 Streatham High Road. The name 'Broadway' was abolished in 1891 and the buildings were allocated to either Streatham High Road or Gleneagle Road.

No. 3 Blakemore Road in 1913, about ten years after the house was built. George Gilbey, the well-known music-hall artist, used to live in this road, where he and his wife were known by the residents as 'Our George and Owd Mill – Darby and Joan'.

Babington Road, *c*. 1906. The road was originally laid out in the 1860s, and former residents include Mr J.W.G. Ross, President of the Royal Warrant Holders Association in 1920, and William Duckworth, Parliamentary Correspondent for the *Daily News* and one of the founders of the London Press Club.

The Grove, Garrads Road, 1907. Located at the junction with Woodbourne Avenue, the house survives today as Saxoncroft Home for the Elderly and can count a number of centenarians among its residents.

Kendal Lodge (*c.* 1920) was previously known as Mindaroo, and can still be seen today on the corner of Garrads Road and Becmead Avenue. It was formerly the home of Eileen Murphy, who was selected by Brian Johnson of the BBC to be one of four women commentators to contribute to Queen Elizabeth II's coronation day broadcast.

Gleneagle Road, *c.* 1910. Developed from 1887 onwards, the road was home to some notable residents, including Hugh Allen, a friend of John Ruskin and engraver of the plates for his books, which were published by Allen's father; John Southward, editor of the *Liverpool Observer*; Martha Corri, premier dancer of the Rosa Opera Company; and Lt.-Col. Frederick Staples, Adjutant General in China.

Gleneldon Road, *c.* 1910. The first houses were erected here in the 1880s. They were built by George Pratt, the owner of the well-known Streatham department store which bore his name. Mr A.B.C. Bellamy, the last Vestry Clerk of Streatham, lived at No. 2, where he died in 1918 aged 79. Lt.-Col. William Lees Greenstreet of the Royal Engineers resided at No. 88.

Harborough Road, shortly after these houses were erected in 1906. The newness of the road is evident from the young trees lining the street. At No. 122 lived a Mr A.G.M. Stubback, who gained some notoriety in the 1920s for discovering a method for preserving cut flowers.

Ivy-clad houses in Leigham Vale, 1910. Originally an extension of Valley Road, the street was renamed in 1896 to avoid confusion. This was one of the few roads in London to be bombed by plane during the First World War when, on 1 July 1917, a bomb fell at the junction with Stockfield Road.

Leigham Avenue, 1916. The dense growth of trees lining this road show how it earned the suffix Avenue. The trees conceal a number of large Victorian mansions that provided comfortable homes for the wealthy residents who used to live here. These included Edward Hodgson, Commandant of the Metropolitan Special Constabulary; Inspector-General Belgrave Ninnis; and the mother of Ray Noble, the famous band leader. The adopted son of Jane Russell, the Hollywood film star, also lived here.

Mount Ephraim Road, *c.* 1909. Building began here in 1864, although most of the houses are of a much later date than this. Among the former residents of this road are Sir William Edmund Pole; David Cox, the artist; Mrs Barbara Barr, step-daughter of author D.H. Lawrence; Arthur Shepherd, whose family owned Hatchard's the booksellers; Edward Stanford, the map maker and seller; and Streatham's first Labour MP, Keith Hill.

Mount Nod Road (*c.* 1914) is named after Mount Nod Farm, which was located by the junction of Leigham Avenue and Conifer Gardens. This farm is believed to be a site of some antiquity and is shown on Ogilby's map of 1675 as 'Mund North Farm'. Among former residents of the road are John Webster, the famous bridge builder; Samuel Yardley, Official Secretary for the New South Wales Government in London in the 1890s; and John Philips, a prolific inventor, who devised the first rotary bacon slicer.

Riggindale Road, *c.* 1908. Most of the houses in this road date from the 1880s. Outside No. 33 in the centre of the picture can be seen one of the last remaining Victorian pillar boxes in Streatham. The Methodist church was erected in 1900 and is a Grade II listed building by Wheeler and Speed.

The junction of Rydal Road (to the right) with Riggindale Road, *c.* 1910. The large houses in Rydal Road attracted many prosperous residents, among whom were Mr L.G. Sharp, Dame Nellie Melba's agent; L.H. Griffiths, champion long distance walker who strode from London to Brighton in 9 hours, 18 minutes, 5 seconds; and a Mr Nicholson, a member of the Royal Household, whose wife did much of Queen Mary's needlework.

Central Streatham

St Leonard's church in the early 1900s. Parts of the old parish church date from the middle of the fourteenth century, although mention is made in Domesday Book of a chapel in Streatham which was probably located on this site. The tall railings were erected around the graveyard in 1830 at a cost of about £480 to deter body snatchers. They were sold for scrap in 1942 for £18 13s 9d to help the war effort.

St Leonard's church, *c.* 1910. Additional seating was provided to accommodate the congregation. The inside of the church was gutted by fire in 1975 and few of the original features seen below survive.

The view from Mitcham Lane, 1908. A warm welcome for Christmas shoppers was the message of the festive decorations strung across the entrance to Streatham's main shopping centre by St Leonard's church. Another banner proudly proclaims 'Streatham for Value' to help boost local trade. In the lower view of the same scene in 1903, without the decorations, the trees towards the centre of the photograph mark the site of The Shrubbery (see p. 156).

The large metal white lion that used to be suspended over the door of the pub of that name can just be seen in the upper view taken in 1908. The imposing building on the left of the lower photograph is the old Streatham police station standing at the junction of the High Road and Shrubbery Road (see p. 138).

Pratts Department Store (*c.* 1910) was Streatham's premier store and the largest shop in the area. It was founded by George Pratt, who began his retailing career at the age of 13 when he worked for William Reynolds, who had a small drapery shop in Bedford Row. When Reynolds retired, George took the business over and under his charge it prospered and grew. In 1867 it moved to new premises called Eldon House, that George had built himself. This building survives today, although its fate is uncertain following the closure of the store in 1990. Note the large gas lights over the windows in the photograph to the right.

The Tate Library. The library (see p. 136) is a familiar landmark on the central stretch of the High Road. It was for many years the terminus for trams journeying to and from London, until the line was extended to Hermitage Bridge in 1909 to link up with the tram services operating from Croydon.

Becmead Avenue and Pendennis Road junction. The top view (*c.* 1916) shows this junction when the two spires on the row of terraced shops leading from Becmead Avenue still had their pinnacles, and large houses still occupied the right hand side of the High Road. By the mid-1930s, when the bottom picture was taken, the spires had disappeared, the northern junction of Becmead Avenue had been redeveloped to provide a new shop called Sharmans (now W.H. Smiths), and the large houses had began to be demolished for commercial redevelopment with the construction of the Astoria cinema (see p. 142).

Woodbourne Avenue to Norfolk House Road. Prior to 1910, Woodbourne Avenue was known as Ena Road, as shown by the name-plates on the side of the building on the corner of the junction in the top picture. Note the domes of the Golden Domes cinema (see p. 135).

The Pump House, *c.* 1919. Latterly known as Laceby's Garage, this building used to stand roughly opposite the Golden Domes cinema and was said to be one of the earliest garages to be established on the A23. These buildings incorporated the old Streatham Pump House, which for many years provided the only source of portable water to the villagers. Up to the mid-1880s the water was delivered with the mail by the local postman, at a cost of three pails a penny.

Mount Ephraim Road junction, c. 1906. A lady and young child are approaching the entrance to The Turret, a large house that stood on the corner of Mount Ephraim Road and Streatham High Road. The last occupier was Dr Knight, a well-known physician in the area, who used to give first aid lectures here on behalf of the St John Ambulance Brigade. The house was demolished in 1932 and the present-day shops and flats erected on the site.

Temperance Billiard Hall, c. 1930. The unusual looking building on the left of the High Road junction with Broadlands Avenue is the Temperance Billiard Hall. This was built in 1928 on part of the grounds of Broadlands, a large grey-brick house that was formerly the residence of James Clark, a plate and sheet glass manufacturer. Part of the hall remains today as the Iceland supermarket.

X This is where I had my 'Photo' taken.

De Montfort House. In the upper view, *c.* 1905, the little girl peering over her shoulder by the lamp-post was just passing De Montfort House and approaching the block of shops leading up to The Horse and Groom public house. Formerly the home of Sandow, the famous strong man, De Montfort House was the headquarters of the Streatham Conservative Party from 1918 until the building was demolished in 1933 and De Montfort Parade erected in its place. The photograph below shows the area in 1913.

Streatham Hill station. About ten years separate these two views, taken from approximately the same position, of the approach to Streatham Hill station. The upper view dates from c. 1902 before Stonehill Mansions were erected on the left hand side of the road. Opposite, the garden wall of Gothic Lodge can be seen. This was a large Victorian house that occupied the High Road junction with Leigham Court Road, and was formerly the home of William Dyce, the famous pre-Raphaelite painter. He was churchwarden of St Leonard's in 1862 and is buried in the parish churchyard (see p. 56).

SECTION EIGHT
Streatham Village

Charles Kennard standing proudly outside his house at No. 93 Wellfield Road, *c.* 1905. The house bears his business sign announcing that the firm of C. Kennard & Son was established in 1875. The family worked as a team, the father doing the building work, while his son, George, did the plumbing. Charles could often be seen in the streets of Streatham riding in his small two-wheeled horse and cart, while his son preferred to cycle alongside.

Sunnyhill Road, *c*. 1906. Formerly known as Leigham Lane, this is one of the old roads of Streatham village. On the right of the top photograph is All Saints' church. Built in 1896, its services were timed so the servants worshipping there were available before and after the services conducted at St Leonard's church, which their masters would attend. The church closed in 1953 and is now used as the Refuge Temple. At the top of the road is The White Lion public house, from the top floors of which the view below would have been seen, with the fields of the Curtis Dairy in Valley Road visible in the distance.

Sunnyhill Road. The top picture, taken in 1907, shows two well-known local traders. W. Allman's beer shop, with its ornate lights overhanging the windows, is on the nearest corner of Farm Avenue. Opposite the coal cart being unloaded are the premises of Francis John Monday & Sons, who had run their upholstery and ironmongery business since the 1870s. Below is Sinclair's newsagents, shown during the First World War. Its windows are crammed with magazines and books, and placards resting against the wall announce the defeat of twelve thousand Turks and ships fighting in the Suez Canal.

Curtis Brothers Dairy, Valley Road, *c*. 1910. The dairy used to deliver bottles of Streatham mineral water with the milk in the early years of this century, and the old well house, built in the early 1800s, can be seen standing in the midst of the dairy in the top picture. The well house survives today and is one of the oldest buildings in Streatham.

Valley Road. The row of poplar trees standing by Curtis's modern dairy building above (*c.* 1930) was a prominent sight in Valley Road and provided a pleasing vista as you journeyed down Sunnyhill Road. The lower picture shows cows leisurely grazing in the fields surrounding the dairy building in 1907. Note the church spires of the Methodist, English Martyrs and St Leonard's churches on the skyline.

Wellfield Road. Prior to 1884, this road was known as Wells Lane, as it led to the mineral wells in Valley Road. This is one of the old village streets of Streatham and originally comprised some fourteen different terraces and cottages, as is evident from the various styles of houses which line the road. Its most famous resident was the comedian Tommy Trinder, who was born at No. 54 on 24 March 1909. The house now bears a Streatham Society plaque, which was unveiled in June 1990 by another famous local comedian, Roy Hudd.

SECTION NINE
Mitcham Lane

The church of the English Martyrs, *c.* 1910. Standing at the junction with Tooting Bec Gardens and Streatham High Road, this church is a familiar sight to travellers journeying down the 'A23 London to Brighton Road. Mitcham Lane is one of Streatham's oldest lanes, and is reputed to have been much improved in the fifteenth century by James Wilford, Master of the Merchant Taylors' Company, whose son left a legacy in his will to help maintain it in memory of his father. The fashionable ladies of Streatham can be seen here carrying their parasols to shade them from the summer sun.

Mitcham Lane, Streatham

Streatham fire station (shown here in *c.* 1915, above, and *c.* 1906, below) was opened in Mitcham Lane in December 1903. Prior to this, the fire engine was housed at No. 45 Mitcham Lane, part of which building still survives today. It is interesting to note that the opening ceremony for the new station was interrupted by the brigade's first emergency call to a fire at No. 149 New Park Road. The right hand half of the station building was destroyed by an enemy bomb on 17 October 1940, which killed twelve firemen and seriously injured three others. The building is now the South London Islamic Centre.

Maber's Hairdressers, *c.* 1927. Members of staff at T.A. Maber's hairdressing salon stand proudly outside their shop at No 15. Mitcham Lane. This establishment catered for both male and female customers and according to the notice above the left hand entrance, also appears to have re-covered umbrellas as a sideline. The building survives today as Tony's Gents Hairdressers.

Plymouth Brethen chapel, *c.* 1922. In the middle of this row of small shops opposite St Leonard's School is the meeting hall of the Plymouth Brethren. At the turn of the century, this chapel attracted around eighty worshippers to its Sunday services. It is currently used as the Kingdom Hall of Jehovah's Witnesses.

Eastern Mitcham Lane, *c.* 1914. This view shows Mitcham Lane from opposite the Thrale Hall Hotel, looking towards St Leonard's School. Note C. Sorby Straw's stables on the right. He was a well-known local riding master and horse dealer and sold bloodstock to King Edward VII, the Prince of Siam and the Emperor of Austria.

St Leonard's School was established in 1813 in a large room located behind The White Lion public house. This was not a very satisfactory arrangement as not only was the accommodation very cramped, but the children also had to endure the behaviour and strong language of the men frequenting the inn. In 1837 the parishioners raised £1,000 to build a new school in Mitcham Lane, next to Miss Kymer's girls' school, and the parish school was transferred to this site in 1838.

Thrale Hall was built on the northern junction of Mitcham Lane and Ambleside Avenue, probably in the early 1860s. Originally a girls' school, in the 1870s it was in use as a 'Hydropathic' establishment and eventually became a private hotel providing a fashionable and popular venue for social events in Streatham at the turn of the twentieth century. In the early 1980s it was converted into a hostel for Chinese commercial and technical experts. It was subsequently demolished and the site developed for housing.

George Blount Home for Roman Catholic Working Boys was located at No. 31 Mitcham Lane before it was removed to Rutford Road. It was opened in June 1907 in honour of George Blount, President of the English Society of St Vincent de Paul, a Roman Catholic philanthropic society.

Carisbrooke College (c. 1930) was situated at No. 55 Mitcham Lane, and was established in 1905 as a private school preparing pupils for public schools and universities. Its aim was 'to inspire a love of right, a sense of duty and a reverence of religion'.

Central Mitcham Lane, *c.* 1908. The upper picture shows the row of small shops that were built in the front gardens of some of the houses located between Aldrington and Thrale Roads. The lower photograph shows the junction at Thrale Road. Note the horse-drawn bus passing the old Streatham Park Hotel and the little boy in his sailor's suit standing on the left hand side of the junction.

St James's church and the Baptist church. Sitting either side of Welham Road, these two churches provide a well-known landmark in Mitcham Lane. The Baptist church was erected in 1902, but the spire no longer exists as it was removed in the early 1960s. The foundation stone of St James's church was laid in October 1909 but the church building was not completed until 1914.

Western Mitcham Lane (*c*. 1909) before the road was surfaced. Note the handsome cast-iron railings on the garden walls of the houses.

The wreckage of a tram involved in an accident at the junction with Southcroft Road on 13 November 1913. The tramcar's brakes failed as it sped down Mitcham Lane and it overturned while negotiating the bend. Fortunately it was not carrying any passengers and the driver, Albert Attridge, escaped injury by jumping clear of the vehicle. However, the conductor, Sidney Mellars, was not so lucky and was badly hurt.

No. 227 Mitcham Lane, 1923. John Newberry, aged 3, is looking out of the ground floor window of his home. He was awarded the DFC in 1944 for his bravery in successfully pressing home repeated attacks in his Mosquito aircraft in support of the advance from El Alamein.

Cosy Corner shops between Southcroft and Edencourt Roads, *c.* 1912. The placards resting against the wall of Martin's, 'The Cosy Corner' newsagents, announce 'Forty Territorials struck by Lightning', the 'Death of the Mikado' and a 'Complete Sherlock Holmes Story' in *Tit Bits*. Note the young boy on the left in the lower photograph with a hoop resting over his shoulder.

West Streatham Streets

Blegborough Road Wesleyan Hall, *c.* 1917. The West Streatham Wesley Mission started in a rented room in Eardley Road in the 1880s. It moved into the mission hall in Blegborough Road in 1903, where it served the inhabitants in the newly-erected houses in the surrounding streets. The mission served the residents of West Streatham for fifty years before it closed down in 1953.

Blegborough Road is named in honour of Dr Ralph Blegborough, who purchased the nearby Fursden Farm in 1824. Building commenced in 1890, but subsequent development was delayed, hence the different style of houses at the far end of the road. Note the tower of the Wesleyan Mission Hall on the skyline.

Corsehill Street, *c.* 1911. Two boys pause from their game of cricket to pose for the photographer. At No. 18 lived Mrs Amy Friesner, who was the oldest of the Tilley sisters, a famous music-hall song and dance act in the 1880s.

Clairview Road, *c.* 1909. This road of fine Edwardian houses overlooking Tooting
Graveney Common was built between 1906 and 1909 on the site of six large mansions,
in one of which, called Woodlands, lived Henry Doulton, the famous potter. He played
an important part in preventing the enclosure of the Common in the 1860s. Doulton
sold his house to Charles Derry, of the famous department store of Derry and Toms,
who lived there until it was demolished to make way for the development of Clairview
Road.

Credenhill Street, 1913. The children on the right are playing in a home-made go-cart. Charles Pepper, known locally as the 'Hermit' because of his solitary existence, lived in this street. Following his death in 1936, his house was found to contain a huge quantity of valuable oil paintings and china, which he had hoarded during his life.

Crowborough Road (c. 1923) was built on the grounds of Furzedown House between 1905 and 1925. The last flying bomb to fall in Streatham exploded at the junction of Crowborough Road and Ramsdale Road on 13 August 1944.

A snow-clad Streatham Road in 1910, when it was just a country lane leading from Streatham to Mitcham. The view is taken from approximately the junction with Ashbourne Road, looking towards Figgs Marsh.

Woodnook Road, *c.* 1910. These modern Edwardian houses were erected in 1907–08. The road takes its name from one of a group of six large houses, which used to stand facing Tooting Graveney Common on the south side of Clairview Road.

Thrale Road, previously known as Green Lane, was renamed in honour of the Thrales of Streatham Park, who entertained there the celebrated lexicographer, Dr Samuel Johnson, as well as other prominent members of mid-eighteenth-century society. Streatham Park was demolished in 1863 and the Streatham Park Estate was developed on the ground. These pictures show Thrale Road in the early 1920s when it provided large comfortable homes for a number of wealthy residents including, at No. 60, Mr Charles Derry, of the famous Derry and Toms department store.

Welham Road. The houses in this street were built between 1904 and 1926, with most of the development being undertaken before the First World War by the local building firm of Swain & Selley. The above postcard advertising the development, offers two-bedroom ground floor maisonettes, complete with kitchen, scullery and bathroom with hot and cold water, at 10s a week, while first floor accommodation was available at the weekly rent of 11s 6d.

Ullathorne Road (*c.* 1905) dates from the late 1870s. No. 3 was one of the three Streatham homes of Mr Charles Derry, of Derry and Toms department store, who moved here from Woodlands (see p. 99) before finally taking up residence at No. 60 Thrale Road. Other former residents include Major-General Percy Holmes of the East Indian Army; Countess Evangeline Dobrski; Sir James Carmichael; Diana Clifton-Park, British ice-skating champion; and George Pratt, founder of Pratts department store.

West Drive, 1909. This road was originally a private road, as can be seen from the notice-board, which warns visitors that it was a 'Private carriage drive – No through passage allowed'. Among those who lived in the large houses which lined the road are Judge Milis Coventry and Edward Wates, of the building firm which bears his family's name, and the local furniture retailers in Mitcham Lane.

SECTION ELEVEN
Streatham Hill

Streatham Hill station, 1908. This view of the station shows the magnificent trees that used to surround the garden of Arborfield, a large house that was destroyed in a Zeppelin raid in 1916 (see p. 48). Following the war, the site was redeveloped with modern shops and flats which heralded the subsequent development of the western side of Streatham Hill.

Streatham Hill bridge, 1906. These photographs show the stretch of road where Streatham High Road ends and Streatham Hill begins. Note the row of single-storey shops built on the bridge over the railway lines which is not strong enough to support taller and heavier buildings.

Leigham Court Estate shops in the early 1900s. By 1905, this row of handsome shops and flats had been constructed on the Streatham Hill frontage of the Leigham Court Estate (see Section Twelve). These were among the earliest buildings erected on the site in order to provide local retail outlets to encourage people to move into the estate. Note the trees and shrubs standing in the front gardens of the large detached houses, which then stood on the western side of Streatham Hill.

Streatham's 'West End'. From the late 1920s through to the mid-1930s the west side of Streatham Hill, between Sternhold and Telford Avenues, was the subject of an ambitious redevelopment project. The large Victorian mansions that lined this side of the road were demolished and the site transformed into Streatham's 'West End', with the Locarno Dance Hall, the Gaumont Palace cinema and the Streatham Hill Theatre erected in their place. These amenities helped establish Streatham's pre-war reputation as the entertainment capital of south London.

The Relay Telephone Company, *c.* 1927. The boy leaning on the lamp-post at the corner of Tierney Road is looking at the Relay Telephone Company's factory that took over the Royal Asylum of St Ann's Society building on Streatham Hill in the early 1920s. This building dated from 1830 and was demolished in 1935 to make way for Pullman Court, which still occupies the site today.

Streatham Hill College was founded by Ernest Blackwell at No. 35 Streatham Hill in 1895. The house was built in 1826 and occupied the corner plot at the junction with Wavertree Road. The sons of 'Bombardier' Billy Wells, the English heavyweight boxing champion, who lived in Nimrod Road, attended this school. The college was demolished in 1936 and Corner Fielde flats erected in its place.

Streatham Hill tram depot stood opposite Telford Avenue and some of the buildings are visible on the right hand side of the upper photograph, which dates from around 1906. Another well-known landmark in the area was the island in the middle of Telford Avenue, which can be clearly seen in these views, and was removed when the road was widened.

The view towards Brixton Hill, *c*. 1903. Looking down Streatham Hill towards Brixton, the road was still lined with private houses, with thick hedges and tall trees providing privacy for the residents. Note the spire of the old Congregational church on the skyline.

Brixton Hill junction, *c*. 1905. The Crown and Sceptre (see p. 133) stands at the junction with Streatham Place. The shop front of Herring Son & Daw, estate agents, occupies the Brixton Hill portion of the junction. The corner part of this block no longer survives today.

Boylands Oak is the large white building visible through the trees at No. 241 Brixton Hill. For forty years this was the home of Kate Carney, the famous music-hall star and comedienne. She lived here with her husband, George Barclay, who ran a successful variety agency from this address. The house was demolished and Christchurch House erected in its place in 1938.

Aspen House (*c.* 1907) was built in 1839 as the family home of the Roupells. Following Mrs Roupell's death in 1878, the house was purchased by William Yeats Baker, the maternal grandfather of Dennis Wheatley, the famous Streatham author. Mr Baker was an avid collector of *objets d'art*, and after his death it took Christies six days to auction off the contents of the house. The building was demolished in 1923 and a tram shed built on the site. This survives today as Stratstone Garage.

Leigham Court Road and Estate

Selborne, No. 18 Leigham Court Road, 1910. In 1836 Beriah Drew, a Bermondsey solicitor, purchased the Manor of Leigham and shortly afterwards opened up Leigham Court Road through the estate. The road was developed to provide large impressive mansions for wealthy and successful businessmen, and much of the early building work was undertaken by George Trollope, the builder, who lived in the road and whose family business later became Trollope and Colls, which survives today as part of the Trafalgar House Group. Selborne, better known today as the Leigham Court Hotel, is one of the few surviving Victorian houses that originally lined Leigham Court Road.

Leigham Court Road just before the First World War, when it was lined with large trees that provided the area with a pleasant rural aspect. The estate office that used to stand on the junction with Knollys Road shows a small and discreet notice on the roof advising 'Maisonettes to Let, Apply Within'.

Heavitree, No. 327, formerly No. 97, Leigham Court Road, 1914. The building was demolished after the Second World War and modern housing erected on the site.

Martley, *c.* 1914. This house, No. 103, formerly No. 33, was typical of the large mansions along Leigham Court Road. It was demolished in 1958, together with its neighbouring property called Leigham Mead, to make way for the building of Dunraven School.

St Peter's church, Leigham Court Road, can be seen through the trees in the top photograph. Work on the church began in 1868 and it was opened for worship in 1870. Prior to this, the congregation met in a temporary corrugated iron building on the opposite side of the road called the Church of St Peter and St Paul. The church was erected on land donated by George Drew, Beriah Drew's son, and the original building was designed by George's son, Richard Drew. The church was considerably enlarged in 1886–7.

Leigham Court Estate was developed from 1891 onwards by the Artisans' Labourers and General Dwelling Company on the grounds of Leigham Court House, a large imposing mansion that was built in the 1830s by John George Fuller, a wealthy banker.

Amesbury Avenue (above, *c.* 1910) and Barcombe Avenue (below, *c.* 1924). These two roads, together with Cricklade and Downton Avenues and Emsworth Street and Faygate Road, formed the major part of the Leigham Court Estate that was popularly known as the 'ABCD' Estate because of the initial letters of the names of these streets.

Cricklade Avenue (above, *c.* 1910) and Downton Avenue (below, *c.* 1924). The houses in these roads still had some way to go to match the luxuriant growth of ivy which had overtaken the walls of the houses shown opposite in Amesbury and Barcombe Avenues.

St Margaret the Queen church, *c.* 1907. Built in 1899 at the Faygate Road junction with Amesbury and Barcombe Avenues, the church served the spiritual needs of the Leigham Court Estate. A parish hall was erected next to the church in 1936.

Hillside Road (*c.* 1912) lies partly in Roupell Park and partly in Leigham Court Estate and contains some fine late Victorian and early Edwardian houses. Mrs Donald Campbell, the founder of the Hitherfield Road Baptist church, used to live at No. 2. Note the weather vane on the spire of the house at the end of the terrace.

Streatham Hill
Streets

Palace Road (*c.* 1904) is named after the Crystal Palace, which moved to Sydenham after the Great Exhibition in Hyde Park in 1851. The road was developed as part of the Roupell Park Estate and was lined with large, impressive Victorian mansions, only a few of which remain today. The gate at the end of the road used to close it off to general traffic. For many years a notice stood alongside the gate stating 'Private Road – Heavy traffic, funerals and hawkers prohibited'.

Christchurch Road, *c.* 1905. The imposing tower of Christchurch can be seen at the end of the road which bears its name. At this time the road was lined with large, detached Victorian mansions that provided comfortable homes for the wealthy merchants and members of the professional classes who mainly resided here.

Drewstead Road (*c.* 1910) was formerly known as Leigham Court Road West. The street is named after Beriah Drew, the Lord of the Manor of Leigham. Among former residents of this road are the widow of Sir Hiram Maxim, inventor of the Maxim machine-gun; the comedian Arthur Rigby; Juan Bonaparte, a descendant of Emperor Napoleon; and Lt. Richard Moore GC, who was awarded the George Cross in 1940 for disarming five mines although he had no practical training in bomb disposal. Sonnie Hale lived at No. 53 (see p. 143).

Two horse-drawn carts enjoy the peace and quiet of Kellieser Avenue at the turn of the century. A number of entertainers have resided here, including Lesley Sarony, the well-known music-hall star of *The Two Leslies* and song writer of 'I lift up my finger and I say Tweet Tweet'.

Local children pose for the photographer in Salford Road, *c.* 1908. The road was so named because the landowner, Mr Lees Knowles, was the member of Parliament for Salford West in 1896 when the street was constructed.

New Park Road, a popular spot for local shoppers, *c.* 1907. Previously known as Balams Lane and Bleakhall Lane, this ancient trackway between Brixton and Balham is mentioned in the Survey of the Manor of Leigham Court in 1547–8. Note the large gas mantle lamps which overhang the windows of some of the shops to illuminate them at night.

New Park Road junction with Palace Road, 1914. Note the gaslight and signpost on the left hand corner, and the bell sign above the Streatham Place post office indicating that telephone calls could be made from the shop.

New Park Road Baptist church was originally known as the Salem chapel. The church was founded in 1840 by ten members of the Streatham Hill Union church. The building was erected in 1842, and opened by the Revd W. Knibb, a well-known advocate of the abolition of slavery in the USA.

No. 74 Palace Road, *c.* 1913. For many years this was the home of Mr Montague Long. This postcard view of the family house was sent by his daughter, Dorothy, to her sister, Edith, at Latimer Rectory in Chesham, Bucks. It informed Edith that Dorothy had just been frightened by a bulldog, which the family kept in a kennel in the garden.

No. 78 Palace Road is typical of the large, detached Victorian houses that used to line this road. This was the home of David Veale, a well-known Irish lithographic artist, who was born in Cork.

Streatham Place at the time of the First World War. The lower picture shows the small row of old shops, which was demolished in the early 1960s in order to widen the South Circular Road. Henry Potter's leech pond used to be situated next to the J.J. Moons public house, formerly The Crown and Sceptre, at the junction of Streatham Place and Streatham Hill (see p. 133). In the first half of the nineteenth century, Potter supplied the London hospitals with around five thousand leeches a year from the pond.

The Telford Park Estate was developed from 1878 onwards on land that formed the dowry of Sarah Kymer, who married Charles Telford, a stockbroker in the City of London, after whom the estate was named. The promotional card above advertises properties available for rent on the estate at £50 to £100 a year, while houses could be purchased from £500. The view below shows the Streatham Hill entrance to Telford Avenue with the Telford Park notice, which used to surround an old tree in the middle of the road junction.

Streatham Pubs

The White Lion, decked with Christmas bunting in 1909. This hostelry, with its impressive façade, was erected in 1895, replacing a much smaller two-storey building built in 1812 that used to have a large white lion standing on the roof. A survey taken in the 1540s shows a tenement called The Lyon on this site. The name of the pub was probably changed to The White Lion in the seventeenth century to distinguish it from The Red Lion (see p. 132). The inn is mentioned in the Surrey Quarter Session records for 13 April 1790 when Charles Copsey was sentenced to be whipped at the cart's tail from The White Lion in Streatham for the space of 200 yd 'until his back be bloody' as punishment for a felony.

The Greyhound, *c.* 1910. At least four different inns of the same name have occupied this site at the top of Greyhound Lane. The one featured above was built in 1871 and replaced a low two-storeyed building thought to have been originally erected in 1730. Mention is made of an inn of this name in the parish accounts of 1726, when 10s was paid to remove a woman and child with smallpox from The Greyhound. This old tavern was much frequented by gypsies who used to camp in Lonesome, at the bottom of Streatham Vale. It was described in 1744 as a 'publick house which is the common rondesvous for all manner of wickedness'. The view below shows The Greyhound shortly after its last rebuilding in 1930.

The Bedford Park Hotel (*c.* 1907) was built in 1882 when it assumed the licence of The Old Five Bells, an ancient beerhouse that used to stand opposite Streatham Green. The foundations of this pub are said to rest on part of the old Roman road.

The King William the Fourth. The inn that has stood on this site for several centuries was originally known as The Prince's Head, assuming its current name in the mid-1800s. The present pub, shown above shortly after its rebuilding in 1904, had as its licensee from 1907 to 1937 Mr Harry Lee, who had two famous sons: Benny, who became world roller-skating champion, and Sydney, a champion billiards player and famous TV snooker commentator.

The Horse and Groom, *c*. 1906. This tavern is said to have been frequented by the Prince Regent for gaming and cock-fighting when he passed through the area on his way to Brighton. In the seventeenth century an inn on this site was known as The Red Lion, and it is shown on later maps as The Halfway House, signifying a stopping place on the road from London to Croydon. The present building was erected in 1865 and was completely refurbished following a severe fire in 1986.

The Manor Arms, *c.* 1925. The original pub to occupy this site was probably erected in the late 1850s or early 1860s and was located a little farther down the road with its entrance facing Mitcham Lane. The present building, shown shortly after it was built, occupies the site of the lodge, coach-house and water tower of Manor Park House, a large mansion that used to stand by Streatham Green and after which the pub was named.

The Crown and Sceptre (*c.* 1919) now known as J.J. Moons. This pub has stood at the junction of Streatham Hill and Streatham Place since 1822. At the turn of the twentieth century the publican was Mr H.B. Hartnell, whose two sons gained great fame in their respective careers. Norman became a royal dressmaker in 1938, designing Queen Elizabeth II's wedding and coronation dresses, and was knighted for his services. His brother, William, an actor, gained world-wide recognition as the first Dr Who in the BBC television series.

The Park Tavern. The photograph above shows the original inn, then called the Streatham Park Hotel, at the junction of Mitcham Lane and Thrale Road. This large three-storeyed white building was probably erected in the early 1870s. It was replaced by the existing building, with its prominent mock Tudor upper storeys, in the early 1930s. Since its rebuilding it has been modernized on a number of occasions, the last refurbishment being completed in October 1992.

Streatham Buildings

Streatham Picture Palace (*c*. 1913) was more popularly known as the Golden Domes. This cinema was opened in 1912 when patrons could see the film *An Actress's Romance*, starring Sarah Bernhardt. The cinema closed down in 1938 and the building became a supermarket in 1967. The site at Nos 130–2 Streatham High Road is now occupied by Kwiksave.

The Tate Library was erected in 1890 as a gift to the people of Streatham by Sir Henry Tate, the sugar magnate of Tate & Lyle fame, who lived in Park Hill, a large house which survives today as St Michael's Convent at the top of Streatham Common Northside. The upper photograph was taken in about 1908. The clock was added to the building in memory of King Edward VII. The lower picture shows the unveiling of the memorial clock by the Mayor of Wandsworth, Alderman Archibald Dawnay JP, on Saturday 5 October 1912.

Streatham swimming baths and assembly rooms shortly after they were opened in 1927. The completion of the building was much delayed by the 1926 General Strike. The baths replaced a large house called Park Lodge, which in the mid-1800s was the home of Lady Feilden.

Streatham postal sorting-office, *c.* 1911. Located in Prentis Road, the sorting-office is seen complete with its courtyard wall and railings, which were subsequently removed.

Streatham police station. The upper photograph shows the old Streatham police station in 1905. It was erected on the corner of Streatham High Road and Shrubbery Road in 1865. By the early 1900s it had become too small to accommodate the increasing number of policemen needed to serve the rapidly expanding population of the area. It was demolished in 1912 and replaced by the present building, seen below shortly after it had been opened later that year.

Streatham Hill station (1913) was the first railway station to open in Streatham. The existing building is little changed today from the one which was erected on the site in 1856. Originally known as Streatham station, the name was subsequently changed in 1868 to Streatham and Brixton Hill station, and then to Streatham Hill station in 1869, to avoid confusion with the modern-day Streatham station.

The old High Road entrance to Streatham station before the First World War. The original station, built in 1868, had its entrance in Station Approach and the High Road entrance was not added until 1905. Note the cab rank outside the station and the Union Jack flying above the house then occupied by the Streatham Constitutional Club.

Streatham Common station was opened as Greyhound Lane station in 1862, the name being changed in 1875. The original building was demolished at the turn of the century and the station which survives today was built in 1902. The top view shows some strange-looking vehicles parked outside the station, probably equipment used by the Volunteer Battalion of the East Surrey Regiment, which was based at the nearby Eardley Road Drill Hall. The aerial view below was taken in the 1920s and shows building work underway on part of the Streatham Vale Estate.

Streatham Empire Picture Palace (*c.* 1912) opened in December 1910. It was one of the earliest cinemas in Streatham and could accommodate 1,200 people. It had a narrow High Road entrance, and a long passageway led customers to the cinema auditorium which opened out at the rear of the building. The cinema was destroyed on 17 June 1944 when it received a direct hit from the first flying bomb to fall in Streatham. The site was subsequently occupied by the Streatham post office until it was relocated to No. 330 Streatham High Road in August 1993.

The Gaumont Palace shortly after it was opened as a showcase for British films on 14 March 1932. The cinema seated 2,431, with standing room for an additional 1,000 patrons. It was closed in the war due to bomb damage, but reopened in July 1955. In 1961 it was converted into Europe's largest bowling alley and survives today as The Megabowl.

The Astoria shortly after it opened to a fanfare of trumpets from the 16th Hussars on 30 June 1930. The 2,500 capacity audience that attended the opening performance saw the 'colour talkie' film *Paris*, starring Jack Buchanan. The cinema has been in constant use and, since 1961, has been known as The Odeon.

Streatham Hill Theatre, *c.* 1930. The foundation stone for this building was laid on 6 September 1928 by Eveleyn Laye, a famous actress, who was married to Sonnie Hale, a well-known comedian of the day and former Streatham resident, having lived at No. 53 Drewstead Road. The theatre cost over £100,000 to build and was opened on 20 November 1929 with the Cochran revue *Wake Up and Dream*, ironically starring Sonnie Hale, who by this time was estranged from his wife. The building is now in use as a bingo hall.

The Locarno Dance Hall was opened in 1929 by Billy Cotton, the popular band leader. It quickly established itself as one of the leading dance venues in London, with many of the country's top bands performing there. Renamed The Cat's Whiskers in 1969, and The Studio in 1984, the building was last refurbished at a cost of £1m in 1990 and is now known as The Ritzy.

The ice rink was opened on 26 February 1931 by the Mayor of Wandsworth, Lt.-Col. A. Bellamy, supported by the local MP for Streatham, Sir William Lane-Mitchell. It was designed by Robert Cromie to accommodate 1,000 skaters and survives today as The Silver Blades.

Streatham Schools

Young scholars at Christchurch School, Streatham Hill, shortly before the First World War. Note some of the boys wearing their bright starched white collars. The school stands to the left of Christchurch, and the original schoolroom, built in 1844, survives today, although it has been much enlarged and altered over the years.

Streatham School (*c*. 1910) was one of the old 'Academies' of Streatham and stood on the High Road between Greyhound Lane and Barrow Road. It was established in 1785 and included among its pupils Sir George Faudel-Phillips, Lord Mayor of London in 1896–7, and, according to local legend, Lord Byron, who is reputed to have carved his initials on an outbuilding in the school grounds. The school was demolished in 1925 and a block of shops and flats built on the site.

Cheltonia College, *c*. 1905. This popular private school was located at No. 45 Tooting Bec Gardens. Prior to 1900 it was known as Sussex House School, whose headmaster, Frederick Arnold, wrote the first published history of Streatham in 1886. The college continued up to 1941 when it was forced to close and the building was used as the headquarters of the local Air Cadets. The house has now been adapted for residential use.

Sunnyhill Road School, *c.* 1906. Built by the London School Board at the junction of Sunnyhill and Valley Roads, the school was formally opened on Thursday 8 November 1900. It was designed by the Board's architect, T.J. Bailey, to accommodate 808 scholars and is a Grade II listed building. Among its former pupils is Hywel Bennett, the well-known TV and film actor.

Granton Road School in the early 1930s. Seen in the centre of this aerial photograph of Streatham Vale, Granton Road School was built in 1928 to accommodate the large number of children then living in the area as a consequence of the development of the Vale Estate.

Eardley Road School (*c.* 1905) was originally known as Mitcham Lane School and was erected in 1894. It is an imposing structure and one of the largest infant/junior schools in the area, originally designed to accommodate a total of 1,020 pupils.

St Helen's School occupied a number of different sites over the years and in 1894 was based at No. 12 Stanthorpe Road. It subsequently moved to No. 394 Streatham High Road, at which address the photograph above was taken around 1900. The picture below shows the girls of the school playing rounders on Streatham Common. In 1929 the school moved from its High Road premises to the former Immanuel church vicarage at No. 22 Streatham Common Northside, where it remained until 1965 when it closed down. The building was subsequently demolished and Javelin Court erected on the site.

St Andrew's School, Coventry Hall, *c.* 1910. This school is sited in Polworth Road and was originally based at Coventry Hall, the large mansion seen in the top picture. This was built at the turn of the nineteenth century by Lord Deerhurst, later to become the Earl of Coventry, on the site of the old Streatham Manor House. Coventry Hall was purchased in 1895 by the Order of the Religious of St Andrew and a convent and school were established there under Mother Marie Xavier, who remained Mother Superior until 1910.

St Andrew's School, Coventry Hall, *c.* 1910. These photographs show the original school building, which was erected in Polworth Road in 1896. The building was subsequently enlarged and modernized. Note the school bell in the upper view, which used to summon the children to classes.

Streatham Hill High School for Girls was based in Wavertree Road, where it still exists today as the Streatham Hill and Clapham High School run by the Girls' Public Day School Trust. The school was opened on 22 February 1887 with seven pupils, who were taught in a building on Brixton Hill. It quickly grew, and moved to a large Victorian house called Courtlands at No: 28 Palace Road, where a junior school is maintained today. Further expansion resulted in the school moving to its existing premises in 1895.

Furzedown Teacher Training College. Furzedown House and grounds were purchased by the London County Council, who established a teacher training college on the site in 1915. The Red House (shown above, *c.* 1934) was built in the same year, and through the trees can be glimpsed the Orangery of Furzedown House. The picture below shows the college dining hall in the late 1920s. Furzedown quickly established a high reputation and was regarded as one of the finest teacher training establishments in the country. The college was closed in July 1978 and the buildings now form part of Graveney School.

Furzedown House (*c.* 1934) was erected in the mid-1790s on the site of an earlier building. The existing house is believed to have been built by Jacob Yallowley, a wealthy banker, following his purchase of the estate in 1793. Among its past owners are Sir John Mitford, who lived here in 1801 when he was Speaker of the House of Commons; Henry Baring, a member of the banking family of that name; and Philip Flower, a successful merchant, whose son, Cyril, became Liberal Party Whip in Parliament and was created Lord Battersea in 1892.

Furzedown Secondary School for Girls, *c.* 1920. Located in Welham Road, this school was opened in 1910 and was known as the County Secondary School. In 1951 it was renamed The Rosa Bassett School, in honour of its first headmistress, Miss Rosa Bassett, who was in charge of the school from its opening to the time of her death in 1925. The buildings now form part of Graveney School.

Furzedown College and County Secondary School in the late 1920s. Many of the surrounding streets have yet to be built. Furzedown House can be seen at the top of the photograph.

The Shrubbery, *c.* 1924. Streatham College for Girls, founded in 1894, was located at this large house, built around 1768 by the Revd James Tattersall, Rector of Streatham. It stood between St Leonard's church and Prentis Road and replaced an ancient building known as the Tyle House, which is believed to have been erected in Tudor times. The picture above shows the rear of the building.

Lady Tate Hall in Prentis Road, *c.* 1914. Opened in 1909 for use by the Streatham College for Girls, the hall was named in honour of the wife of sugar magnate Sir Henry Tate, who presented the building to the school. Following the closure of the college in 1933, the hall was acquired by the local Jewish community and since 1938 it has been the South London Liberal Synagogue.

SECTION SEVENTEEN
Aerial Views

The magnificent view of Streatham and the surrounding area from the high ground at the top of Streatham Common in the 1930s. Before the erection of tall blocks of flats and offices, only the spires of local churches and the tower of Manor Park Lodge thrust above the trees and houses which formed the suburban skyline.

Factory Square, *c*. 1928. The tall chimney stack on the left marks the P.B. Cows Indian Rubber manufacturing complex based at Factory Square. Behind the chimney can be seen the old Streatham silk mill, built in 1820, which survives today as part of the Sainsbury's supermarket which now occupies the site. To the right of the mill is Immanuel Church School, and at the bottom of the photograph Streatham Modern School can be seen, looking very much the same as it does today.

Coventry Park Estate in the late 1920s. The Chimes, overlooking the war memorial at the corner of the High Road and Streatham Common Northside, can be clearly seen towards the centre. Behind this building is Coventry Hall surrounded by open ground on which Albert Carr Gardens was erected after the Second World War. The old Streatham Bus Garage can be seen on the other side of the High Road next to the United Reformed church.

Streatham station, c. 1928. The large Victorian house in the bottom left hand corner was formerly Wandsworth Council offices, before the building was demolished to make way for Streatham swimming baths. The large building at the foot of Ambleside Avenue was Streatham Hall. It was here that Dame Edith Evans, then aged 22, made her first appearance on stage in October 1910 when she played Viola in the Streatham Shakespeare Players' production of *Twelfth Night*.

Central Streatham towards the end of the 1920s. The three spires of St Leonard's church, the church of the English Martyrs and the Streatham Methodist church are clearly visible.

Streatham High Road, looking towards the police station from the High Road junction with Mitcham Lane, *c.* 1900.